PAMPHLETS ON AMERICAN WRITERS • NUMBER 78

UNIVERSITY OF MINNESOTA

Erskine Caldwell

BY JAMES KORGES

D1286937

UNIVERSITY OF MINNESOTA PRESS • MINNEAPOLIS

813
C143k

© Copyright 1969 by the University of Minnesota
ALL RIGHTS RESERVED

Printed in the United States of America at
Jones Press, Minneapolis

Library of Congress Catalog Card Number: 71-625289

Am

PUBLISHED IN GREAT BRITAIN, INDIA, AND PAKISTAN BY THE OXFORD
UNIVERSITY PRESS, LONDON, BOMBAY, AND KARACHI, AND IN CANADA
BY THE COPP CLARK PUBLISHING CO. LIMITED, TORONTO

ERSKINE CALDWELL

HUNT LIBRARY
CARNEGIE-MELLON UNIVERSITY

JAMES KORGES, who has taught English, is employed by Control Data Corporation. He edits *Critique: Studies in Modern Fiction*. In addition to technical writing he has published many essays on diverse writers and on Portuguese, Flemish, and Japanese fiction.

↙ *Erskine Caldwell*

Lıke most best selling authors, Erskine Caldwell tends to be patronized or ignored by academic critics and serious readers. Many know of *Tobacco Road* and *God's Little Acre*, but tend to dismiss them as merely popular or salacious novels. Few seem to know the full range of the man's work: his text-picture documentaries, such as the remarkable *North of the Danube*; his charming books for children; his neglected *Georgia Boy*, a book that stands with Faulkner's last work as one of the finest novels of boyhood in American literature; and his short stories, some of which rank with the best of our time. A brief study cannot fully redress the indiscriminate neglect of readers and critics (nobody will argue that all Caldwell's works are valuable, or that all need to be considered at length); but I will indicate briefly the achievement of Erskine Caldwell, in an attempt not only to do justice to the writer, but to prevent if possible another disgrace in American letters: the sort of disgrace we visited on Melville, forgotten for years; the sort of disgrace we seem to be visiting on Phelps Putnam, Delmore Schwartz, and other good poets now almost entirely out of print, as well as on Glenway Wescott (who remembers that first novel, so highly praised by Ford Madox Ford?).

The specter of Faulkner, the ways we patronized and misunderstood his work until it was honored abroad and claimed by us all, is sobering, especially when one recalls his famous list of the best contemporary writers: Wolfe, Faulkner, Dos Passos, Caldwell, and Hemingway. The list infuriates admirers of Hemingway, their man being last; critics of Faulkner worry that their man should be second; and others are annoyed by the absence of

Fitzgerald, Steinbeck, Farrell, and so on. In all this disputation, however, hardly anybody elects to notice that Caldwell's name is there or to wonder about the body of writing Faulkner admired.

Younger readers dismiss him as a writer of the *old* pornography, for how tame, demure, almost tidy seem the passages that were read aloud in courts as evidence of Caldwell's obscenity, back when he was America's most banned writer. Younger critics seem unwilling to read Caldwell with care. For example, John Bradbury, in his 1963 volume, *Renaissance in the South*, says of Caldwell: "Furthermore, Caldwell's flat style, his insensitivity to subtleties of fictional presentation, allow him no means to redeem the crude vulgarities he delights in recording." One might take Bradbury's evaluation seriously if Edwin Granberry, Kathleen Crawford, Patti Hill, and Edyth Latham did not get fuller treatment than Caldwell.

The "flat style" Bradbury dislikes is called by others "plain style." When a writer of a complex, involuted, rich, moving, powerful prose, like Faulkner's, goes out of his way to praise a lean, spare, direct, plain style, like Caldwell's, we do well to pay attention. In *Faulkner at Nagano*, Faulkner answered a vague question about Caldwell: "For plain, simple style, it's first rate. There was a thought or a certain moving power and quality in his first book, *Tobacco Road*, but after that, it gradually grew towards trash, I thought. But in the first book there was a very moving power . . . human and moving, even though I never did quite accept them as actual people." *Tobacco Road* was not Caldwell's first book, and Faulkner leaves unexamined the serious problem of accepting literary creations "as actual people." But he did try to point out the central fictional accomplishment of Caldwell, as at the University of Virginia where he said that "The first books, *God's Little Acre* and the short stories, that's

6

enough for any man, he should be content with that, but knowing writers, I know he's not, just as I'm not content with mine."

Few people are satisfied with the work they do in a lifetime; the greater the attempt, the greater the dissatisfaction. Yet, obviously, though a man may never be wholly content, he need not be wholly discontent. That much of Caldwell's work "grew towards trash" does not alter the fact that Caldwell has produced an important body of work in both fiction and nonfiction.

Erskine Preston Caldwell was born on December 17, 1903, in the small settlement of White Oak, Coweta County, Georgia. His father, a well-known Presbyterian minister, was moved frequently from congregation to congregation, partly because of his liberal views which irritated Georgia crackers, and partly because of his talents in settling problems within congregations. This early travel afforded young Caldwell with observation of people and places, of motive and action, of countryside and human nature. His mother, thought by some to look too youthful to be a preacher's wife, tutored him at home, though he later received formal education at Erskine College in South Carolina, at the University of Pennsylvania, and at the University of Virginia. He left the University of Virginia without taking a degree and began working as a newspaper writer. In 1925 he married Helen Lannegan, with whom he had three children. He left Georgia in 1926 to settle in Maine and to begin seriously to write prose fiction. His jobs over the years have been diverse: cotton picker, stagehand, seaman, cabdriver, professional football player, bodyguard, cook and waiter, book reviewer, lecturer, editor, motion-picture script writer in Hollywood (1933–34, 1938, 1942–43), and foreign correspondent, in addition to his work as writer of novels and short stories.

Caldwell's early stories came to the attention of Max Perkins, the great editor at Scribner's who brought along the talents of

Wolfe, Hemingway, and Fitzgerald. Perkins, like other editors to whom Caldwell submitted manuscripts, rejected many stories; but unlike the other editors he saw reason to encourage Caldwell to keep writing. Finally he accepted some of Caldwell's stories set in northern New England for publication in *Scribner's Magazine*. Gradually, Caldwell's work, under the encouragement of Perkins, began to be published in many magazines and journals and to be included in the annual anthologies such as O'Brien's *The Best Short Stories* and the *O'Henry Memorial Award Prize Stories*. Scribner's published his first two important books, the collection of short stories *American Earth* and the novel *Tobacco Road*. The relationship between Caldwell and Perkins was strained by an argument about the manuscript of Caldwell's next novel, set in Maine, and Caldwell left Scribner's for Viking Press. He finally came to agree with objections to the novel, and instead of pressing for its publication he wrote *God's Little Acre*, his masterpiece. His first collection of essays on social problems appeared in 1935. In the same year he was introduced to the celebrated photographer Margaret Bourke-White with whom he did the famous *You Have Seen Their Faces*.

In 1938 he lectured at the New School for Social Research before leaving the United States to be, in 1938–39, a newspaper correspondent in Mexico, Spain, and Czechoslovakia. While in Czechoslovakia he collected material for *North of the Danube*, a book which again combined the prose of Erskine Caldwell and the photographs of Margaret Bourke-White, who became Caldwell's second wife early in 1939. Caldwell traveled in China, Mongolia, and Turkestan in 1940. In the next year he happened to be in Russia when Hitler invaded and was thus one of the few American correspondents to report that phase of World War II firsthand. On his return to the United States he began to edit the *American Folkways* series of regional books (1941–55). In

1942 he married his third wife, June Johnson, having one son with her. His present wife, Virginia Fletcher, whom he married in 1957, did the line drawings which illustrate *Around about America*, one of his more recent books of travel and observation. Caldwell is a novelist of "the old school" in that he does not earn a living by reporting on political conventions for a magazine or review, does not teach "creative writing" at a university, does not have a separate income from a medical practice or a position in a bank or insurance company. Nor is he one of those "writers in residence" at a university who reside a lot but publish less and less. Erskine Caldwell is a professional novelist, who also produces works of personal observation.

Caldwell's autobiography, *Call It Experience: The Years of Learning to Write* (1951), begins in backwoods obscurity and hardship, but when it ends with Caldwell the best selling novelist in publishing history autographing pocketbook editions of his works in drugstores, the shape of the story is the classical shape of the world's great autobiographies. A good autobiography is, contrary to what the general public may think, not just the story a man tells about his life; autobiographies are, when well written, stories of transformation or conversion, from St. Augustine whose confessions begin in cosmopolitan vice and end in a triumph over that vice and a coming to Christian virtue, to André Gide's *If It Die . . .* which ends abruptly after his successful conversion from conventional bourgeois son to cosmopolitan homosexual. Caldwell's autobiography of his public life as a writer is a book about recognition, about the transition from the poor boy from the provinces to the wealthy man whose determination and talent enabled him to transcend humble beginnings. It is a classic American life, the very embodiment of one version of the American Dream. Yet he has successfully avoided the danger of autobiographical writing: alienation of the reader. St. Augustine had to lead up to and away from that episode in the orchard with great care so as not to appear self-righteous; Gide had to exercise subtle control over his material and his readers' responses to prevent immediate revulsion from his story of how he found happiness with his boyfriends; Caldwell had to guard against his readers' admiration for success, admiration which is also touched with envy. Caldwell keeps the narration swift, freighting it with a large portion of verifiable fact and of anecdotes which are lively and not self-centered. Indeed the straightforward report of his many tribulations with ignorant but powerful censors, whether at the level of small-town librarian or of state board, is not self-pitying. It is calm in tone and even good-humored.

Call It Experience has raised for some readers a difficulty, however, in that Caldwell himself says that in the early novels he wanted "to write about Southern life as I knew it." Such remarks lead some readers to assume the novels to be journalistic reporting, or factual social studies, or naive realism. One recalls the same sort of confusion that resulted when Faulkner remarked in an interview: "I write about the people around Oxford." Literary tourists flocked to Oxford to see how many characters they could identify. But writers tend to give these simple, even misleading assertions, so that we must, as D. H. Lawrence insisted, trust the work rather than the writer's statements about it.

To understand Caldwell fully and thus to illuminate his best books as well as to prevent oversimplification, one needs to know the early *The Sacrilege of Alan Kent*. The book is made of three sections, each separately published: "Tracing Life with a Finger" (1929), "Inspiration for Greatness" (1930), "Hours before Eternity" (1931) — titles significantly different from those of the other short novels published during the same years: *The Bastard* (1929) and *Poor Fool* (1930). Kenneth Burke in his remarkable chapter on Caldwell in *The Philosophy of Literary Form* calls this early work a "sport," in that it is so different from other works by Caldwell. The book is closer to a series or a collection of Joycean "epiphanies" than to a novel or collection of three stories. The numbered paragraphs, some as short as a sentence, are about what is remembered and about the tricks of memory as the central character recalls moments made sharp by intense feeling, whether of pain or joy. The moments are not idyllic; the tone is often downright grim: life is a sacrilege, we live in pain and hurt.

One section (II:8) sounds like the beginning of a film by Ingmar Bergman: "I lived for a while in a room with two girls. Neither of them could speak English nor understand it, and I never knew what they were talking about." That rich scene is left in this epiphanal form, as in Hemingway's figure of a short story as an iceberg, only a small amount actually showing. In Caldwell's notations, most of each story is left unstated. Occasionally sections sound like the "deep images" of Robert Bly, James Wright, and other members of the "Sixties" group, as in II:11: "Once the sun was so hot a bird came down and walked beside me in my shadow." At the end of Part II, the narrator returns to his hometown, but the place is inhabited by strangers except for a girl whose "breast was bursting like a blossom in the warm sunshine."

Part III follows the central character through a winter journey and various odd jobs, including a carnival in which Caldwell, with a great imaginative stroke, has the fortuneteller go crazy. Repeatedly the images lie in one's mind and are suddenly transformed — as in the scene in which the central character sees a girl so beautiful that the sight of her beauty scars his eyes (III:8). One recalls a later work, James Dickey's remarkable poem on faces seen once only. The section contains a good deal of fine ribald humor which foreshadows later plot devices. In III:17 an employer keeps Negro girls for his satisfaction, until one girl defeats him: "The man brought another Negro girl to the house but she had greased her body with lard and he could not hold her." That is the essence, the reader being left to add the usual details of a great tall story in the manner of Twain or Faulkner — the Negro girl lowering herself to the status of greased pig to maintain her higher conception of herself. But that is part of the submerged iceberg, part of the unspoken available.

The book is strange, at times brilliant. Caldwell would not again use this method, except in passages of description in the novels and in pointed details in the essays, as when in an essay in *Some American People* he places an action in perspective by syntactical means: the scene is North Dakota, the time is August 1934, the action is "The Last Roundup" in which the federal government in two days cleared the Badlands of ten thousand head of cattle, shipping them to pastures not destroyed by drouth: "The last great roundup is over, the bones of the culls that fell by the wayside have been picked clean, and the painted canyons of the Badlands are unchanged." *The Sacrilege of Alan Kent* is one of the books we must look to if we are to understand Caldwell's full range and his place in contemporary literature.

His first novel, *The Bastard* (he says he did not select the title), is as weak as some of the more recent novels; yet it is important: it suggests later themes and techniques that give such rich comic effect and insight to his best fictions. *The Bastard* is a novel about chance and control, rendered in various ways: the chance of a man's birth and the ways he may control his life despite his birth; games of chance like craps and of control like pool; chance meetings with women and carefully planned seductions; the chance of falling in love and the willed rapes and murders. The absence of characterization reinforces the theme of chance; but that absence also damages the book. Not a good novel, it contains fine touches: when Sheriff Jim betrays his steady at the whorehouse by getting married to an out-of-town girl, that girl infects him, his son, his boarder, and the neighboring men with syphilis. The disease is the blight descended on the community when its ruler breaks the code. In another fine, though less mythic, scene a naked and drunk woman leads a mule to the courthouse demanding the animal's arrest "for insufficient rape." These scenes are, however, the high points in the story of the bastard, Gene, violent, lusty, immoral, criminal. He marries, fathers a deformed child, commits infanticide, and wanders away, dispossessed, alienated, alone: the very image of modern man in more recent fiction. He has some of the vain self-consciousness exemplified by Meursault in Camus's *The Stranger* and some of the pompous egotism of Sergius in Mailer's *The Deer Park*. But Caldwell's book is slight, more important, perhaps, for its place in the development of the clichés of alienation in modern fiction than for its literary art.

Poor Fool is a story of fighters and fixed fights. Things just happen, as people just drop dead in the novels of E. M. Forster, and as accident and coincidence are often crucial in the fiction of Thomas Hardy. Yet in this story of chance, love, and death, fights are fixed. The point of the story is that the fights, a metaphor for competition in a "free" enterprise system, are fixed by Mr. Big and that Mr. Little is a "poor fool" for trying to fight the system and bring Mr. Big to justice. Incidental episodes are again the best parts of the book, although the novel shows some of the structural strength that will characterize Caldwell's later work (even an admittedly bad book, like *The Last Night of Summer*, 1963, is almost classical in the purity and force of its structure), and although the themes here tentatively examined will later give power and force to better novels.

Next to these early fictions, probably the least well known

HUNT LIBRARY
CARNEGIE-MELLON UNIVERSITY

works by Caldwell, and thus the most neglected, are the books he did with Margaret Bourke-White. The neglect is unfortunate since although the neglected early fictions are interesting mainly as forecasts of things to come, these text-picture books are some of the finest examples of that genre. The tradition of the text-picture book goes back, in America, at least as far as Jacob A. Riis who published in 1890 *How the Other Half Lives*. The Caldwell and Bourke-White books belong to a five-year spurt of talent in this genre. Their first, *You Have Seen Their Faces*, was published in 1937. Then in 1938 Archibald MacLeish published *Land of the Free — U.S.A.* which is, as he says, "the opposite of a book of poems illustrated by photographs. It is a book of photographs illustrated by a poem." Dorothy Lange and Paul Taylor published *An American Exodus* in 1939, the same year that Caldwell and Bourke-White published what may be the masterpiece of their collaboration, *North of the Danube*. The astonishing year for the genre was 1941 when Caldwell and Bourke-White published their superb *Say! Is This the U.S.A.* and James Agee and Walker Evans published their celebrated *Let Us Now Praise Famous Men*. The Agee-Evans book has been reissued; unfortunately the rest remain out of print. Successful text-picture books are rare, depending as they do on the accidental harmony of two workers in different media, like the rare conjunction of composer and librettist which leads to grand opera.

In pictorial art, commentary is superfluous; yet iconographic content may be located and may be pointed by commentary. The collaboration of Caldwell and Bourke-White resulted in a group of books in which prose and photograph are in harmony and have a single object, the captions and essays focusing our reading of the pictures, the pictures illuminating what we see in the prose. Both picture and text depict image or situation in moral terms, the moral being in image or situation, with only muted

14

editorial diction in most of the prose and only discreet editorial lighting in the photographs.

In *You Have Seen Their Faces* a Negro boy and his hound stand framed in a doorway, the interior walls of the shack papered with pages from magazines. The "white" advertisements comment ironically on the poverty of the place and its furnishings, and of the lives lived there. One notices the framing doorway, the side lighting from a hidden source in the room beyond, the control of shadow, and more. Yet if we look at this moving composition only as an arrangement of light and shade, we miss the point. Caldwell's caption (and the essay that goes with this section of photographs) helps focus our eyes: "Blackie ain't good for nothing, he's just an old hound dog." The captions do not turn the photographs into anecdotes or literary imitations; but they help achieve a full response to the photograph, as the photographs help achieve a full response to the essays. A caption such as "Bringing the white-boss's fine cotton along" seems banal enough; but its simplicity keeps it from competing with the photograph, and its meaning prevents us from seeing the great photograph as just a study in vanishing points and sky, which it also is. We are led by the prose to those small figures in the field, to a sense of human misery in the midst of visual beauty.

An eloquent photograph of an old man's face in Arkansas: "I used to be a peddler until peddling petered out." A grim-faced woman with a child: "Snuff is an almighty help when your teeth ache." And a lined, leathery face: "I've done the best I knew all my life, but it didn't amount to much in the end." As compared with the remarks of "Existentialists," usually well-fed men in comfortable jobs teaching well-fed students, the "existential" dimension of these text-picture books is staggering: the determined, often even fierce animal urge toward life, even under the most humiliating circumstances, mocks Camus's celebrated remark in *The Myth of Sisyphus* that suicide is the only serious philosophical problem left us. (Some "Existentialists" forget that Sisyphus led a vile, mean, cruel life and got no worse than he deserved.) The withered-limbed, starved-minded, puff-bellied, illiterate bastards — redneck, nigger, poor-white — in this book live, perhaps incapable of a sophisticated notion like suicide; for suicide seems a luxury these American peasants could not afford.

The essays in the book argue for a government commission to investigate and propose remedies for the moribund agricultural system in the South. Southerners were outraged by the book, Donald Davidson attacking it in his famous essay-review in the *Southern Review* by saying that the South could never cure its wrongs if people kept drawing attention to those wrongs, especially southerners: "What is the matter with any Southerner who turns state's evidence under circumstances like these?" What seemed wrong Davidson indicated by saying that "as a student of farm tenancy in the South Mr. Caldwell would make a splendid Curator of a Soviet Park of Recreation and Culture." Given the slowness of progressive action in the South, such a commission might have been able to accomplish something by 1968 when Senator Robert Kennedy found illiteracy and actual starvation in Mississippi — conditions that, once revealed, shocked a nation.

You Have Seen Their Faces was an extension of Caldwell's famous essay on tenant farmers, later reprinted in *Some American People*, and of his lectures at the New School. His argument for correction of social and economic evils went unheeded. Indeed things have not changed much for the impoverished tenant farmers; except that as T.R.B. in the *New Republic* for June 8, 1968, remarks, the absentee landlords now find it profitable to forbid tenants in Alabama the use of land on which they once raised corn and vegetables for their own consumption. Landlords can make money on those garden plots by leaving them unplanted and collecting a subsidy from the government for adding that land to the "soil bank." In the year when the Hawaiian Sugar Company got $1,353,000 for not planting crops, babies were born dead in Mississippi because pregnant women could not afford even minimal diets. Unfortunately, in 1937 Caldwell's prose effected only the rage of Donald Davidson, rather than remedies.

One of the best of the text-picture books composed by Caldwell and Bourke-White, the one Caldwell is fondest of, is *North of the Danube*. Images of camera and language record and report on Czechoslovakia, its edges ceded to Germany and Hungary. It was a place of great scenic beauty; a place of towns, such as Uzhorod, where cars were rare, bicycles were ridden by Ruthenians, Czechs, and Germans, while Jews and gypsies walked; a place in which the sun shone, crops grew, and one generation followed another in a social structure that had changed little in five hundred years. Caldwell treats all this tenderly but without sentimentality.

In the last of the Caldwell and Bourke-White text-picture books on an American theme, *Say! Is This the U.S.A.*, the prose is so clean, almost coldly dispassionate, that one at times almost forgets to notice the reportorial point of view, the implied judgment; just as one at times tends to overlook the moving content of Margaret Bourke-White's photographs, they are so stunningly composed and lighted. This book contains almost no overt editorializing, and does not argue a case as *You Have Seen Their Faces* did. Both text and photographs are starkly objective, but the opinions of writer and photographer are implicit in what they elected to report.

The movement of the book is rich and varied, from commonplace jobs and filling-station sociology to "land-cruising" whores and rich boys out for a thrill; from a wry report on why cattle raisers keep one goat around their horses and cows to a sympa-

thetic view of the problems of a schoolteacher instructing children in an "Americanization" class; from a man trying to scrape
up a dollar so his wife and kids can go to the picture show to
a manufacturer of electrical equipment in Illinois who argues
that war in Europe must be kept going for the sake of America's
industrial growth; from good country folk in Soso, Mississippi, to
a batch of titillated ladies in Cedar Rapids, Iowa, each fancying
herself the prototype of Carl Van Vechten's now almost unread
but once notorious *The Tattooed Countess*. Caldwell's range of
tone and effect is impressive. He gets the tone of a street-corner
evangelist, a pompous lieutenant colonel in the cavalry, a B-girl
trying to get a job, a Rotary Club luncheon, and the majestic
peevishness of a secretary trying to locate her boss by telephone.
The book is neither a broad and balanced historical account of
the United States in 1941 nor a penetrating sociological treatise;
rather it gives a sense of a nation's movement, the live sense of
place and person rendered in prose and photograph, unadorned,
clean, and effective.

The essays in another early book, *Some American People*
(1935), also afford entry into Caldwell's world, a sense of the
range of his literary art, and a direct presentation of the moral
views which inform his novels. The section "Detroit" is a fierce
and bitter account of old Henry Ford's empire, that automobile
industry being, to Caldwell, "one of the clearest examples of
industrial slavery." Then from the abuses of industry the book
moves in its final section to "Southern Tenant Farmers" who are
"living under decivilized conditions." As "straight" economic
and sociological analysis these two essays may be damaged by
Caldwell's outrage at inhumanity; but the essays are all the more
valuable for that outrage. They are in the central tradition of
polemic, and like all great polemics they survive the special circumstances of their creation. Things now have changed in De-

troit, but the essay is still witty and moving, still a brilliant document illuminating both one aspect of a period in American history and one aspect of man's use of man. And the essay is still valid, as "A Modest Proposal" is still valid though Ireland is free from absentee English landlords.

As with some of Hemingway's journalism, some of Caldwell's reports could stand as short fiction. An anecdote in the "Cross-Country" section titled "Grandpa in the Bathtub" is a satisfying whole in itself, reminding one of more recent works of fiction and of the theater of Ionesco. The anecdotal report concerns an old man who hoards rainwater until he has ten gallons: "I've never seen so much water since '96." He moves all his furniture into the bathroom in a show of the affluence of poverty, and as though it were his last act in life, he bathes, joyously.

The book contains many scenes of people who because of the vitality of their despair would survive bleak days and hungry nights. In the "Prefatory Note" for the Decennial Edition of *Tobacco Road*, Caldwell writes of people he saw as a boy wandering around the South: "They believed in cotton. They believed in it as some men believe in God." At the end of the note he sums up the history and the theme: "First, tobacco, and then cotton; they both had come and gone. But the people, and their faith, remained." This is the stark survival of the unfittest in an economic system like that that made the plot of Gogol's *Dead Souls* possible. These people have the stubborn dignity of "surplus miners" who would be all right, one man in *Some American People* suggests, if they "could find something else to do, if they had unemployment insurance to live on, if they removed to South America, or if they committed suicide." They are "wound-up, finished, done," but they survive with a fierce animal will that underlies the desolate characters in Caldwell's great stories, and gives his characters their dignity and vitality.

A later book of nonfiction, *In Search of Bisco* (1965), uses the search for a boyhood friend to structure a report on travel and people. Its superficial structure is a collection of nonfiction short stories; but the book also has a thematic structure. Time, law, and race recur, like motifs in music, the interaction of the three being the book's major theme.

Time is sometimes almost Proustian: Caldwell is literally try- ing to find (or find out about) Bisco, his Negro boyhood play- mate; but in the search for that past friendship, he finds the realities of the present, and he has intuitions about the future. Time is for some speakers in the book history; or time is what works on law; or time is what we try to get through, without too much trouble. For some, the passing of time is traced in the gradual lightening of the Geechee Negroes' color; and we are reminded of the past, of the beginnings of this history of racial strife, by the still shiny coal-black of the Gullah Negroes, a dark- ness maintained by economic causes. So, in the complex narrative, the very colors of skins come to symbolize the delicate interac- tion of economics, race, time, and law.

The first chapter sets up certain themes in three scenes, for Caldwell is, in his reporting as in his novels, a great scenic artist. He recalls three Negro boys: Bisco, from whom he was separated when he got too old to sleep in Bisco's bed in the Negro shack; Sonny, lynched for alleged relations with a promiscuous white girl; Roy, sentenced to two years on the chain gang for supposed- ly stealing an iron washpot too heavy for a man to lift. The white community, to preserve its code, (a) separated friends, and (b) lynched one Negro and imprisoned another by extralegal means. These early sections prepare for later reports on the civil rights movement in which the Negro community, to gain its rights, (a) makes friends, or tries to ("You can't make anybody be your friend by pulling a knife or pointing a gun at him"), and (b) when necessary uses extralegal devices to achieve ends. The southern whites ignored laws to work injustice; southern Negroes took to ignoring laws to work a justice denied them. Active violence of rednecks was met by passive nonviolence of Negroes. And in this struggle of race and law, time is on one side.

These books of report and record are for the most part effective; but the propaganda of Caldwell's wartime books is difficult to judge. The text-picture collaboration of Caldwell and Bourke-White, *Russia at War* (1942), is a valuable record bringing together photography and reporting they did during the war, much of it for *Life*. The commentary is often predictable propaganda about Russia, our wartime friend, but often anecdote and incident blood the propaganda. Caldwell was also Moscow correspondent for the CBS radio network and the newspapers *PM* and *Daily Mail*. From his dispatches and a diary he made two other books published in 1942, *Moscow under Fire* and *All-Out on the Road to Smolensk*. Both record, in that lean and unobtrusive style, sights and sounds of Moscow, the small incidents which most accurately reveal the tension and calm of a great city under attack. Other scenes are a "natural" for Caldwell, like absurd images of fifty-ton tanks ramming head-on, ammunition having been exhausted. The machines of destruction are turned helplessly on their backs, like monstrous turtles. The other book of 1942 is a disappointing novel, *All Night Long: A Novel of Guerrilla Warfare in Russia*. The plotting is tight though episodic, but the characterization is perfunctory, being divided between Russian hero and German swine. On the other hand, the set speeches are effective pieces of rhetoric within the conventions of propagandistic fiction — a set of conventions as yet insufficiently studied, and in many ways as arbitrary and as strict as the conventions of courtly love poems.

Caldwell's talent seems to falter in the longer forms when he leaves a southern setting, as in the war novel and in *A Lamp for Nightfall* (1952), a novel set in Maine and dealing with old ways threatened by outlanders. Some of the short stories, like the celebrated "Country Full of Swedes," succeed in northern settings; but his major fictional accomplishment lies in what Caldwell refers to several times in *Call It Experience* as "a cyclorama of Southern life." This "cyclorama" is unlike Faulkner's mythical county; and if we try to understand Caldwell's cyclorama in terms of Faulkner's county we will end by misunderstanding both men. Faulkner composed a sort of history, the novels linked in various ways to give an incredibly rich fabric of lives and events. It is, nobody doubts, one of the highest moments in Western literature. Caldwell was not after that sort of complex historical fabric, but after scenes and actions that embodied themes and types in the present.

His "cyclorama" consists of ten volumes: *Tobacco Road, God's Little Acre, Journeyman, Trouble in July, Tragic Ground, A House in the Uplands, The Sure Hand of God, This Very Earth, Place Called Esterville,* and *Episode in Palmetto.*

Tobacco Road (1932) did not become a best seller (indeed sales barely covered Caldwell's advance) until after its dramatization by Jack Kirkland, a play which almost closed after two weeks but managed to survive to become so popular that for years it held the record of longest consecutive run on Broadway. *Tobacco Road* is about tenacity in the spirits of men and women deserted by God and man. The book is not about tobacco or Georgia, about sexology or sociology, but is instead a work of literary art about the animal tug toward life that sustains men even in times of deprivation. The grandmother is one of the central symbolic figures in the book, hovering in the background, lighting a fire in the stove in that great primitive faith that a fire will bring the god, and that a god will provide where men fail.

Life's major vital signs are eating and sexual intercourse, the two motives wittily, grossly, and magnificently rendered in the famous opening section of *Tobacco Road*: Lov with his bag of turnips which are the object of Jeeter's desire, Ellie May wanting Lov's body, Lov being had on all counts as Negroes stop in the road to watch the high-life of the poor whites. This mockery of desire in two of its forms (eating and intercoursing) begins a series of mockeries, such as the mockery of that old-time religion as it is embodied in its modern apostle, Sister Bessie; the mockery of that old-time plantation system, now degenerated into tenant farming, embodied in the absentee landlord "Captain" John; the mockery of the clean-cut wholesome boy who plays ball and is interested in cars, embodied in the simple-minded Dude who almost knocks the house down by chunking his ball against it and who becomes the child groom of Sister Bessie just to get a car to wreck; the mockery of hospitality in the splendidly funny and sad hotel scene in the city where hospitality becomes lust as Sister Bessie is shifted from room to room, to the delight of all.

The book is also a study in relationships and desertions. Man in this symbolic landscape is frustrated in his relationship to the soil because fertility has deserted the land. The sterile relationship of man to land is paralleled in the sterile marriage relationship of Lov and Pearl, in the stupid lust of Sister Bessie for Dude, in the failure of the whole family to speak to the old grandmother — that is, to have a right relationship with the past. The grandmother is a choric figure of silence, commenting by her presence rather than by any words. The currently popular discussions of "failure of communication" as a theme in modern literature have themselves failed to consider the poignance of the theme in *Tobacco Road* which is almost a novel of silence: no letters come from absent children because there is no rural delivery on the tobacco road; for years Ada did not speak to her husband, and in the course of the novel Pearl will not speak to hers; Jeeter speaks in monologues, usually not addressed precisely to anybody. Once when Jeeter tries to command Dude to quit knocking the house down with his baseball, his injunction goes unheeded. These peasants are the very opposite of the vessels of goodness and wisdom envisioned by Wordsworth and Tolstoi.

In *Tobacco Road* as in *God's Little Acre* the house itself, symbol of family and permanence, is in danger. In the later novel, the house is in danger of sliding into one of Ty Ty Walden's holes, the symbol of his lust for gold literally undermining the symbol of family. In the earlier novel, the house is in danger from the aimless play of the younger generation, and at the end of the novel is victim of a southern tradition, that of burning off the weeds and saplings each spring. The aimless destruction of this traditional fire, erroneously said to kill boll weevils, in the turning of a wind destroys the now aimless lives of Jeeter and Ada. The fire destroys the house, but cannot purge the land of accumulated sin and degradation, burning, burning in *this* wasteland.

Yet there is something grand about thieving, lazy, immoral, stupid old Jeeter; and the physical deformities of the harelip girl and the woman without a nose are symbolic deformities. Indeed one suspects that literary historians will gradually see Caldwell in relationship with Flannery O'Connor as a writer whose characters were often deformed not for the purposes of sensational fiction or sales but for purposes which allow the writer to explore, whether under the tragic mode or the comic mode, spiritual conditions. When Jeeter says of God that "Him and me has always been fair and square with each other," and that "I don't know nothing else to do, except wait for Him to take notice," *Tobacco Road* takes its place in a body of modern literature which includes both Samuel Beckett's *Waiting for Godot* and Simone Weil's *Waiting for God*.

24

Erskine Caldwell

God's Little Acre (1933), despite its reputation as comic pornography, is no more an "exposé" of southern mentality or habits than the typist-at-teatime section of *The Waste Land* is about unfair employment practices in London. It is a novel of rich sexuality, sexuality being in this symbolic landscape, as grim and spectral as the Hollywood landscape of Nathanael West's *The Day of the Locust*, the one impressive life-sign. Yet just as the farm produces neither cotton nor gold (except for the crops raised by the Negro sharecroppers on their part of the land), so no woman in the novel is pregnant, despite all the sexuality. Darling Jill is blunt about not wanting to marry until she is "a few months gone." No marriage is in sight, though, despite the complaint of her rotund suitor that she has been "fooling with a lot of men." Pluto Swint's complaint gets a characteristic reply from Ty Ty Walden, the proud father: "I'm tickled to death to hear that. Darling Jill is the baby of the family, and she's coming along at last." Few responses have been so disarming and such high wit since Lady Bracknell confessed herself glad to hear that Ernest smoked. Ty Ty is a great believer in men and women doing what God made them to do — a Georgia cracker's sort of argument from design. He remarks that Darling Jill is "just made that way. It don't hurt her none, not so that you will notice it, anyway." At the end of the novel Darling Jill will marry the great fat man, even though she is not pregnant. After all, that they should marry seems part of God's plan, being acted out on God's little acre; and if things go wrong, brother killing brother, that must be part of God's plan too. This impossible paradox is one of the central themes of the novel, often most powerfully rendered in sexual terms, as when Pluto says: "It's a pity God can't make a woman like Darling Jill and then leave off before He goes too far. That's what He did to her. He didn't know when He had made enough of a good thing."

It might be read as an exemplum on the natural goodness and natural depravity of man; or, especially those sections set in the mill town, as a document on labor relations at a particular time in American history; or as a broad rural comedy parodying in the manner of recent "black comedy" the notion that farmers live close to the soil, uncorrupted by the devious ways of society and civilization, and so are the salt of the earth, the backbone of of American life; but *God's Little Acre* can be read more meaningfully as a novel about dream and reality, power and impotence, the force of life and the force of death. The characters are studies of how single-mindedness of purpose or desire shapes people and compels them to behave in certain ways as economic, sexual, political, or theological agents. Ty Ty Walden, for instance, in his habitual insistence on being "scientific" in his obsessive digging for gold is as "hobby-horsical" as any character in *Tristram Shandy*. Each character in *God's Little Acre* is identified by and with his driving motive. Ty Ty Walden and his son-in-law, Will Thompson, the central male characters, each has a dream and each wrecks his life and the lives of others with that dream, comically and selfishly in the case of Ty Ty, tragically and altruistically in the case of Will. The two characters are possessed by a yearning to find in deadness and dust (the sliding red dust of Ty Ty's holes or the yellow dust of the mill town into which abused workers spit) the sources of power, of value, of some other kind of life; and part of the darkness of Caldwell's vision of life, bitterly rendered in comic terms, is that these yearnings are defeated as they are acted out either in the withered pastoralism of Ty Ty's farm or in the dehumanized urbanity of mill town or big city.

The dreams of the characters are obsessive and the actions extravagant; yet the literary effect is of order and inevitability. The relation of destiny and personality in the working out of the plot is more complex than previous critics have conceded, just as the range of characters is more complex. The novel has been pigeonholed as a product of some sort of deterministic naturalism or pornographic local color; but clearly it is not that. Rosamond's acceptance of the death of her husband, Will, as inevitable is an expression of the fatalism that haunts the book; yet his death will come at the hands of either the husband of one of the women he elects to seduce or the company police he elects to defy, so that fate is the working out of man's will. The relationship of Moira, Tyche, Hubris, and Hamartia has been the central theme in Western literature, and is no less the theme of *God's Little Acre*, though here presented mainly in Christian terms of God's plan and divine will in relation to the flawed nature of fallen man. Toward the end of the book, after the ruined land has been polluted by blood (Numbers, 35:33), Ty Ty expresses a peasant's version of man's tragic position on the Great Chain of Being: "There was a mean trick played on us somewhere. God put us in the bodies of animals and tried to make us act like people. That was the beginning of trouble."

The characters have often been dismissed by critics as ignorant, lecherous, exotic, and so on; but the novel is structured on a series of contrasts arising from distinctions in characterization. The three brothers Walden, for instance, illustrate different types of son; and the son most often ignored in reductive critiques of the novel is Shaw, the quiet and kindly bachelor. He is silent when taunted by his father, not because he is stupid but because he is understanding. He is the only male in the novel who respects the taboo on incest. He is the one who sees that the Negro share-croppers are fed, who remembers what he learned in school about the difference between placer mining and lode mining, and who at the end of the book must report to the sheriff that his brother Buck has killed his brother Jim Leslie. Though a shadowy character, his presence helps undercut the notion that Caldwell's world is populated exclusively by dumb lechers.

The structure and tone of the novel have also been ignored. The action of the book begins in a slow slide of reddish dust and clay over Ty Ty's feet, and rises to a classic double climax of plot and subplot. This action takes place in a symmetrical seven-part structure, distinguishable by changes in setting: farm, mill town, farm, Augusta, farm, mill town, farm. The chapters about the action in Augusta are at the center of the plot and contain the turning point, after which the tone of the book begins to change. Repetition, for instance, is one of the common devices in comedy, and Caldwell uses it to achieve some of his finest comic effects. But gradually repetition of phrases or tags, like Pluto's "and that's a fact," cease to be funny. Rosamond's repetition of "yes" and "yes, I know" is fatalistic and pathetic. Toward the end of the book, repetition reaches lyric intensity in the work chant of the Negroes, and tragic intensity in the insistent threats and commands of Buck and Jim Leslie during their final encounter, when repetition becomes an index of inflexibility of attitude and motive. Early in the novel Pluto's blinding of a lizard with tobacco juice is echoed in an almost archetypal scene in which Darling Jill blinds Pluto with a handful of suds for having greedily stared on her nakedness as she bathed; but late in the novel, repetitions and echoes become ritualistic, as when the corpses of both Will and Jim Leslie are mourned over by the same three women. One begins to lose some of the condescending assurance a reader normally has in the presence of comic types, and to become aware of the bitter quality in Caldwell's humor. For example, Ty Ty's constant shifting of God's little acre, the portion set aside for God, is one of the mechanical repetitions that becomes funnier on each occasion. Yet at the end of the novel, after Buck, Cain-like, kills his brother and flees over the newground, Ty Ty realizes that he forgot to shift the acre, and that the murder took place on God's portion. The son who died and the son who fled are the old man's tithe; and the novel ends with one last shift of the acre, as Ty Ty sends it after his fleeing son, so that he will be eternally on God's little acre.

Caldwell's concentration on sex and economics has led to misunderstanding, readers criticizing him as they criticize Alberto Moravia for not presenting "higher" aspects of man. Moravia is quoted in Del Buono's book on him as saying: "My concentration on the sexual act, which is one of the most primitive and unalterable motives in our relation to reality, is due precisely to this urgency; and the same may be said of my consideration of the economic factor, which is also primitive and unalterable, in that it is founded on the instinct of self-preservation that man has in common with animals." The astonishing effect of many of Caldwell's novels results from his merging of violence and humor, theology and economics, diet and sex. We have no precise critical terminology to describe exactly that effect.

The dietary and sexual themes are, of course, related. I am not suggesting reduction of characters to the menus in the novels ("What these men had to eat and drink/ Is what we say and what we think" is true; but the formula is, as John Crowe Ransom well knew, wittily reductionist), yet recent evidence of starvation and dietary deficiencies in Mississippi seems to indicate another reason for the lethargy and stupidity of some of Caldwell's characters. An inadequately nourished brain does not develop; deprivations in diet lead to deprivations of mind. The caloric dimension of ethics is a theme in these novels, as it is in some plays of Brecht. American audiences perhaps best know the theme in the statement in *Three-Penny Opera*: first give us bread, then morals. The standard meal in *God's Little Acre*, besides the inevitable chicory for breakfast and an occasional watermelon, is grits and sweet potatoes, with once in a while a piece of ham and maybe some biscuits with sorghum. In the novels of Caldwell's later period the scene moves to the city where people seem better fed, so that food becomes a point of wit instead of need. In *Gretta* (1955) the couple on a honeymoon is in a dilemma about whether to eat or copulate; and in another scene a man "explains" to Gretta how to overcome loneliness, the image being culinary: " 'You take two slices of bread — one's you and one's me — and then you put something in between — that's company. See how easy the whole thing works out?' He leaned against her and smiled." In *Close to Home* (1962) a good deal of the humor hinges on a man's love for his freedom as that love is tested against the greater love for cold sweet-potato pie for breakfast. Eating becomes part of the comic presentation of ethical problems.

A good deal has been made of the special values of the family as the unit of society, as the element most likely to give stability to a social order, and so on. One of the most celebrated fictional embodiments of this attitude is Ma Joad in John Steinbeck's *The Grapes of Wrath*. Caldwell's Ty Ty Walden in *God's Little Acre* also values family, though Caldwell and the characters in his novels tend not to be as somber about it as either Steinbeck or the Agrarians. Ty Ty tries to keep his family together, arguing that his younger son ought to stay away from the corruptions of the city: "There ain't no sense in a man going rutting every day in the whole year. . . . He ought to be satisfied just to sit at home and look at the girls in the house." Later Ty Ty and Will both excuse even incest itself with the homely wisdom: "It's all in the family, ain't it?" The decadent family in *A House in the Uplands* (1946) sinks to sterility and disintegration, since disintegration of family is also a good, though the simplistic arguments in behalf of family and "tradition" would not admit it.

Likewise in *This Very Earth* (1948) the old grandfather is like
Steinbeck's Ma Joad until toward the end of the novel. Then he
has a superior intuition: instead of trying by any means to hold
the family together, he helps the family splinter; since each mem-
ber had different aims and goals, trying to hold the family together was to impose a willful and womanishly possessive wish
on a variety of people. This realization comes too late, as the
realization of Oedipus, for instance, comes too late; thus the old
man is frustrated in his insight, and dies suddenly at the sight of
murder in his house, Noble Hair's murder of his wife. The old
verities (the farm, coon hunting, family) do not serve.

In *God's Little Acre* the richly comic presentation of family
activity on the farm is contrasted with the unproductive struck
mill town and with the brutality of the big city. The family goes
to Augusta to try to get money from the son, Jim Leslie, who
denies his father and who is married to a barren and diseased
woman, though she is "rich as a manure pile." The emotional
poverty of the city folks is set off against the richness of feeling of
the impoverished country folk, free from the economic meanness
of making good marriages or of charging for sex, like the Augusta
whores who try to take Ty Ty. This contrast, so important in the
thematic development of *God's Little Acre*, may be indicated in
another way by comparing two scenes, one from this novel and
one from the later *Gretta*. In her confession scene, Gretta tells
her husband about her compulsions to seduce men and to per-
form a ritual preliminary to copulation: sitting on the floor to
remove voluptuously her stockings, asking the man for money,
and then kissing the man's genitals: "I can't help it. It's like
being thirsty and wanting a drink of water — it's like being
hungry and craving something to eat." Gretta's homage to the
phallus is compulsive and selfish, whereas Ty Ty Walden's appre-
ciation for female beauty and the great generative principle is

31

quite different. He praises his daughter-in-law Griselda's "rising beauties" and says that "the first time I saw you . . . I felt
like getting right down there and then and licking something.
That's a rare feeling to come over a man, and when I have it, it
does me proud to talk about it for you to hear." Whereas Gretta's
kiss is a sign of homage, like the adoration implicit in those
monumental stone phalluses on Delos or the adoration women
of Pompeii gave statues of men with erections, that kiss is put
in the context of Gretta's degradation, and so is itself degraded.
Ty Ty at no time touches Griselda, his adoration being ironically
"pure." He praises perfection of female flesh and acknowledges
great admiration: "That's the way, and it's God's own truth as
He would tell it Himself if He could talk like the rest of us."

God is not absent from *Gretta* but He tends to be the object
of supplication, as in Gretta's prayer: "Please, God, let it be that
way — forever . . . . Please, God, please!" In *Tobacco Road* and
God's Little Acre there is not this longing and supplication, but
rather an admission of God's omnipotence and an acceptance of
what He has deemed fit to give His creatures. This point is, it
seems to me, overlooked by Chester Eisinger when in *Fiction of
the Forties* he complains that *The Sure Hand of God* (1947) "suggests by its title the operation of divine providence, but the
determining forces in this novel are social and biological." The
overlooked point is that God works, if at all, through the biology
and society of His creatures.

Journeyman (1935) has been taken as a sensational novel at-
tempting to expose certain religious exoticisms in the South.
Though the book seems slight, its wit and irony make it a charming and effective fiction. The action occupies six days constituting
a fragmented Holy Week. As in fashionable metaphysical poetry
the man of religious feeling finds imagery and ecstasy in sexual
happenings, so in *Journeyman* the man of sexual feeling finds

imagery and ecstasy in religious happenings. The book opens on
Wednesday with the arrival of Preacher Semon Dye, a name play-
ing yet again on the sexual pun on "die." He arrives not like
God in a whirlwind but in a car that backfires, emitting black
odious smoke that drifts onto the porch and into the house. The
satanic sign is obvious, though wholly realistic in origin. Clay
Horey, the farmer being visited, is outraged: "Damn the man
who'd do that right in the front yard!" Semon Dye does not
bring spiritual renewal to the grim lives of Clay and the other
inhabitants of Rocky Comfort; but he does bring renewal of
vital life-signs. Indeed his approach to souls is wonderfully
physical. He gooses men ("Good God Almighty!" Clay shouts
when Semon gooses him) and strokes the buttocks of women,
explaining that "it's just like stroking the wildness out of a colt.
You can't do a thing with them until you stroke them some."

Semon arrives on Wednesday to have supper with Clay and
to "have" a fetching Negro girl. He plans a revival meeting, to
be held in the schoolhouse since the Rocky Comfort church had
long since been turned into a guano shed, perhaps reminding us
that Christ himself was born in a stable. Semon inverts the acts
of the New Testament. Instead of driving moneychangers from
the temple, he is expert in getting money; instead of a chaste
relationship with Mary Magdalene, he offers to pimp for one of
Clay's wives. (Clay has had five wives, taking another when one
wanders away, being a bit taken aback when one wife returns
unexpectedly: "It makes me feel sort of foolish to be sitting in
the house with two of my wives. And, on top of that, it might
be against the law, or something.") Indeed Semon manages to get
Clay to pay a dollar to lie with his own fourth wife, then gets him
to bet his fifth wife in a crap game which Semon wins. Semon is
a shrewd man who also happens to be a man of God — a "lay"
preacher, as he says. He does not deliver from temptation but

brings it; nor give daily bread but takes it; nor forgive debts but makes his host his debtor.

Friday night is occupied with a grandiose bed scene as Semon, having won Dene in the crap game, learns of her disgrace. She has loved and slept with a Negro man. This powerful sin requires a powerful rite of purification which Semon administers with the most trusty instrument of his ministry: " 'I love the Lord!' she screamed in the dark room."

The entombment on Saturday (Semon having "died" in Rocky Comfort) is suggested when Semon and Clay find Tom, the "spirit" man (maker of the finest "Georgia dew"), at his favorite place: in a cowshed, sitting on a stool, looking out a crack in the wall. There is nothing but woods to see, but somehow looking at nothing through a crack in the wall is better than looking at nothing. Tom says: "I come down here and sit and look, and I don't see nothing you can't see better from the outside, but that don't make a bit of difference. . . . I don't know what it is, and it might not be nothing at all when you figure it out. But it's not the knowing about it, anyway — it's just the sitting there and looking through it that sort of makes me feel like heaven can't be so doggone far away." This is the rustic southern notion of "beyond" that Robert Frost expressed in a rustic northern poem, "Neither Out Far Nor In Deep." The trinity of hillbillies huddle in the dark of the shed, looking out the crack in turns, getting drunk on "dew." Tom sums up their response: "That's the Goddamnedest little slit in the whole world. . . . I can't keep from looking to save my soul." And indeed he cannot.

After this grand scene comes the long Sunday revival service, ending in an autoerotic orgy as Semon Dye helps the congregation do what is indicated in these sects by the phrase "come through." (*You Have Seen Their Faces* contains some photographs of people "coming through.") The whole congregation is possessed by the Holy Spirit which leads the people to speak in tongues (glossolalia) and to writhe in mystical surrender to a jerking rapture. On this Sunday of this inverted Holy Week, everybody comes to life, the women in violent agitation and the men "prancing up and down like unruly stallions." Nor is anybody much surprised that Semon Dye is not to be found in Rocky Comfort on Monday. These people need no angel to tell them "He is not here."

The conclusion is abrupt and apt. The novel is funny and delightful, being one of three remarkable books Caldwell published in 1935: *Journeyman*, the essays in *Some American People*, and a fine collection of stories in *Kneel to the Rising Sun*. The only other year in Caldwell's career that would be quite so rich was 1940 when he wrote one of the most important of the text-picture books, *Say! Is This the U.S.A.*, and published both a major collection of short stories, *Jackpot*, and his next novel, *Trouble in July*.

Chapter Six of *Trouble in July* contains an incredible comic scene. By an almost Elizabethan ruse, a bed-trick is brought off when the outraged wife jabbers after discovering her husband, the sheriff, locked in a jail cell with a colored girl, as at the same time serious lynchers talk serious business. The mixtures of dialogue, the absurdity of the situation, the fierce intensity of one set of characters played up by the hopeless bumbling of another set, combine to make the scene grandly funny and grandly terrifying. All the while the mulatto girl sits in the cell, silent and observing, like a conscience.

The story focuses on the incompetent sheriff and on his desire to do the will of the white people rather than to impose the will of the law on them. The plotting is tight and the study of the vagaries of human desires (legal and economic as well as sexual) is often penetrating. But some of the best things in the novel

are the presentations of interior states of the characters by means
of description of natural detail. When the sheriff returns, the
restoration of order in their relationship is signaled by the odor
of cooking food, even before he sees his wife. Later in *Claudelle
Inglish* (1958) an adultery is accompanied by the odor of cut
clover, odor being used to give a sense of both distance and
presence, since the betrayed husband in the field cuts the clover. When, in *Trouble in July*, the girl who falsely accused the
Negro boy of raping her is rejected by her white suitor, who
calls her "nothing but a cotton-field slut," she realizes that she
has made a mistake — not because she told a lie and got a Negro
lynched, but because as a dishonored woman she is no longer fit
to be a white man's wife: "The sun was going down, looking as
though it had suddenly grown tired after the long day. Towards
the east the country was beginning to look cool and peace-
ful. There was a small dark cloud drifting towards the sun on
the horizon. In a few moments the cloud began turning crimson
and gold as the sun's rays struck it. For an instant the whole
western sky looked as if the world were on fire; then the sun sank
out of sight, leaving the cloud dark and lifeless. The air moved a
little, for the first time that day, and the branches on the trees
swayed, rustling the dark green leaves." The girl "grasped her
arms full of weeds and bushes. She had to have something to
hold onto." Later, the almost ritual stoning to death of the girl,
beneath the hanging corpse of the Negro boy, is presented dis-
tantly, as the sheriff sees stones in the air and hears sounds: "A
piercing scream filled the woods. A roar of angry voices followed. A bluejay fluttered recklessly through the branches of a
tree overhead and, screeching shrilly, disappeared." The sheriff
"walked to the bank of the branch and stood looking at the water
swirling under a fallen log."

Almost wholly neglected in discussions of Caldwell's work,

since it does not fit the stereotypes of violence or sexuality into which his novels are usually placed, is what may be his finest book, *Georgia Boy* (1943) which stands with Wright Morris' *My Uncle Dudley* and with Faulkner's *The Reivers* as one of the most delightful and satisfying evocations of a past time in which man and boy had a relationship of joyful innocence and uncomplicated freedom. Caldwell's book is invention rather than recollection, for the "my old man" of *Georgia Boy* is not at all like the Reverend Ira Sylvester Caldwell whose life and relationship with his son are tenderly and lovingly evoked in another of Caldwell's best books, *Deep South: Memory and Observation* (1968). This recent book of nonfiction adds substantially to the rather austere accounts of the Reverend Mr. Caldwell in such works as *The Centennial History of the Associated Reformed Presbyterian Church* (Charleston, 1905), and adds to that information previously available Erskine Caldwell's sense of the vitality of life and the moral tone which informs his best novels. *Deep South* is important in its own right, but it is also important because it makes clearer the power of his inventiveness and imagination, as demonstrated in *Georgia Boy*.

Georgia Boy is an episodic novel, almost a collection of very closely related short stories, in which a complicated adult relationship is presented through the first-person narration of a twelve-year-old boy. The book is dominated by four characters: the boy, William Stroup, who narrates the story and who is himself dominated by his mother although he is wholly devoted to his father; the mother, Martha, who is steady and sane, taking in washing to support herself and her son, trying to inculcate in the boy the middle-class virtues of niceness, hard work, and social acceptance; the father, Morris, who is eccentric, inventive, free, a lusty sporting man who comes up against the restrictive world of women so often that he is led finally to speculate that "the

37

good Lord ought never put more than one woman in the world at a time"; and the Negro help, Handsome Brown, who is the boy's friend and the helpless pawn in the competitions of Martha and Morris, and of man and nature. Handsome Brown stands for all the fall guys in the world, having to go up onto the roof to get some goats down, having to return some boots bought with money Pa Stroup got in one of his harebrain schemes, having to go up into a sycamore tree to chase out the shirttail woodpeckers which subsequently mistake him for part of the tree and act accordingly. He is *that* "close to nature." He is docile and dumb, as one kind of Negro tends to be in the southern landscape of Caldwell's novels; but the reader is led to accept him as the boy narrator does, or as Huck accepts Nigger Jim.

One strain running through many of Caldwell's best stories, though perhaps not part of his conscious intention, is a sort of reply to Thoreau, especially to Thoreau's preoccupation expressed in the chapter from *Walden* titled "Where I Lived, and What I Lived For": "Simplify, simplify, simplify." The characters in Caldwell's stories have often simplified their lives, and they live close to nature. Indeed in *God's Little Acre* Ty Ty Walden, whose name obviously suggests the Sage of Walden Pond, does exactly what Thoreau advised: "if one advances confidently in the direction of his dreams, and endeavors to live the life which he has imagined, he will meet with a success unexpected in common hours." Ty Ty Walden, Will Thompson, and Jim Leslie Walden each "advances confidently in the direction of his dreams" and each is destroyed by the realities of life. The two best novels Caldwell has written, *God's Little Acre* and *Georgia Boy*, are both radical criticisms of the American Dream of ingenuity, self-reliance, rugged individualism, and the virtues of determination and doggedness. In *Georgia Boy* the narrator innocently admires the ingenuity of his old man who, once he has a political appointment, makes success his goal. Of course the political appointment happens to be as dogcatcher and of course the boy's old man succeeds in catching lots of dogs by offering them meat and getting them to follow him; but success is success, and after all the officer was only doing his duty. When the boy's old man decides to become a financial success by baling waste-paper and selling it, he is wholly devoted to his work, baling not only old newspapers and such, but even his wife's recipes, her dress patterns, Sunday school hymnals, and finally her love letters. Whether he is collecting scrap metal, ringing the churchbell, or tickling the local grass widow with a feather, the boy's old man is single-minded; and the boy's report is always admiring and enthusiastic, which leads to some grandly absurd reports, as in his blandly factual report of the time his ma caught his old man in the woodshed with a visiting gypsy queen: " 'Shut up!' Ma said. 'Where are your clothes?' " The success of the episodes as humor rests on just this enthusiastic report of things the boy does not understand. The pacing of the episodes, the blending of comic pathos and broad humor, and the suggesting of serious themes through naive report are all the result of flawless han-dling of the point of view. The whole book culminates in one of the funniest and saddest episodes, as ma has her way with the old man's fighting cock, College Boy. The episode is called "My Old Man Hasn't Been the Same Since" and it is one of the finest tales in modern American writing.

After *Georgia Boy* Caldwell began the second group in the series of novels with southern settings. *Tragic Ground* (1944) is about hill people moved to town to work in a munitions plant in World War II. As the title indicates, the very ground is tragic, the ground of a wartime white ghetto called "Poor Boy." As one character remarks, "the finest folks in the world would get mean and bad if they had to live in a place like this." The book contains some of Caldwell's good ribald humor, but the tone is predominantly grim. A social worker functions as a sort of *deus ex machina*, but is a futile one; for as soon as some families are moved out of the ghetto, others arrive, characters who can say about themselves, "I was born poor and I'll die poor, and I won't be nothing but poor in between." Such characters may seem unreal to affluent readers; but they are related to the realities of poverty many Americans began to become aware of only when they read Michael Harrington's *The Other America*. It is this other America which is, in Caldwell's novels, the tragic ground. *A House in the Uplands* (1946) has the powerful theme of the decline of a once prominent family, symbolized by the physical decay of the house and set off by the rise of a new breed of men who believe in law and order. But despite some aphoristic dialogue and some brilliant descriptive touches, the novel remains a poor treatment of a great theme. Most of the novels in the second part of the "cyclorama" (those after *Trouble in July*) tend to treat important themes but also tend to sensational plotting and trite characterization.

Typical is the last novel in the series, *Episode in Palmetto* (1950), a comic melodrama with didactic intent showing how the intrusion of a sexually attractive and frank young woman, a schoolteacher, brings to the surface and to a climax the latent violence in a small town. The plot, tightly constructed to take place in a single week, centers on the uses the town makes of sex, from the random lusts of unhappy husbands to the power plays of jealous and ambitious wives who use sex and gossip as weapons. The novel shows these motives, so important to the adult life of the town, developing in the schoolroom, where a girl falls in love with the young teacher and when repulsed attempts to destroy the teacher; and where a boy falls in love with the teacher, but because he cannot learn the rules of deviousness and hypocrisy — the rules which make seduction and adultery possible in the adult world — he destroys himself. The procession of suitors and the profusion of jealousies lead to an attempted murder and to suicide, resulting in a good deal of "schooling" as each character learns some kind of lesson — even the young teacher whose cruel self-discovery is that she enjoys promiscuous sexuality. The comic and brutal scenes are played by characters like Reverend John Boykin Couchmanly; Pearline Gough, the rejected schoolgirl; Em Gee Sheddwood, the farmer who needs a wife to care for his children; Cato Pharr, the mail carrier; Milo Clawson, the principal who reprimands the teacher for wearing a tight yellow sweater, but who is anxious to speak to her in private; and Jack Cash, the one-pump filling-station attendant who each year courts the new schoolteacher, but who this year flees in a torment of nervous agitation when the teacher mischievously offers to sleep with him. Unfortunately the wit and broad humor, as well as the social comment on small-town life, are mixed with a good deal of superficial psychological comment and superficial motivation.

Race relations have become one of the central themes in Caldwell's more recent novels. The earlier treatments had been unsuccessful, as in *Place Called Esterville* (1949), or had been brief and ironic, as in Jeeter Lester's remark in *Tobacco Road* that "Niggers will get killed. Looks like there ain't no way to stop it," or Clay's remark in *Journeyman* that he "don't mind seeing a dead darky once in a while." Such remarks depend for their effect on the separation of the character speaking them and the author, as in that famous exchange in Chapter XXXII of *Huckleberry Finn*, when Huck explains to Aunt Sally what happened: " 'We blowed out a cylinder-head.' 'Good gracious! anybody hurt?' 'No'm. Killed a nigger.' 'Well, it's lucky; because sometimes people do get hurt.' "

In one of the recent good novels, *Close to Home* (1962), a reader is aware of the grotesquery of Native Hunnicutt's marriage to a fat woman fifteen years his senior, Maebelle Bowers, and of his spending his wedding night hunting possums. But this deliciously comic beginning is set off against the tender and loving devotion of Native's relationship with the Negro girl Josene. Likewise, the grotesque murder of the Negro boy Harvey (he is castrated and made to strangle to death on his own testes) is set off by the quiet dignity and justice of Josene's interview with her white father, a successful lawyer and director of the bank. The complex texture of the novel results from Caldwell's blending of humor and melodrama, his modulation of tone and speech rhythm, and his supporting of didactic intent with dramatic incident.

In his most recent novel, *Summertime Island* (1968), he has written a didactic romance narrated by a boy of sixteen who comes of age one summer at a fishing camp on an island in the Mississippi River. The story, slighter and simpler in texture than Caldwell's other recent novels, is another telling of the timeless story of a boy's coming knowledge in a symbolic setting. The "set speeches" of the adults in this novel have irritated some readers. They are long and didactic but they are in character. Certainly one mark of the relationship of generations is that older men tend to monopolize any "dialogue" they pretend to have with sixteen-year-old boys. *Summertime Island* is unsatisfying not because of "set speeches" but because of Caldwell's failure to utilize the point of view. First-person narratives are, of course, of different kinds. In *Georgia Boy* the narrator is a boy who naively reports the scene; but in *Summertime Island* the narrator is a man remembering when he was a boy ("I was almost sixteen years old then") at some time vaguely in the past (women's skirts were almost to their ankles, fire trucks had solid rubber tires, and the town had gravel paths instead of paved sidewalks). The difficulty is that the narrator, once he begins telling the story, must pretend to recall lectures and long speeches and to report them as though he were a boy again. The reader must suppose, if he can, that the now mature narrator can tell the story without seeing that his uncle is a drearily pious bore, or without seeing that his incestuous aunt is little more than an incredible wish fulfillment. Had Caldwell let the mature narrator come to terms with the full implications of what he reports about the past, the novel might have been one of his finest.

Perhaps the best of his novels since *Georgia Boy*, *Miss Mamma Aimee* (1967), is about the live past and the dead present. Tradition and family history are rich and alive, but the land is being sold off to support a moribund remnant of past glories. Times are changing, for the family, for race relations, for traditional values. The novel is structured on a complex series of reversals, even the final revelation of mother-hate which balances mother-love. As Aimee awaits the arrival of the horny preacher, Raley Purdy, a taxi brings Connie, her "baby girl" who is now a prostitute. Frustrated expectation, an ancient comic device, is here used with great symbolic effect. Miss Mamma Aimee Mangrum is the victim of contradictions implicit in her names, and she is the focus of the reversals: once her name was good for any amount of credit, but now she must try to give a bad check to the gas-station attendant, Gene Infinger, who refuses it. The preacher's manly looks attract women, but he blushes at flattery, and when he sees a girl naked he worries about what "if Billy Graham saw me now." The girl asks, "who's Billy Graham," to which he replies, "I can't talk about Billy Graham when you're stark naked — he wouldn't want me to." After which she strips him and goes to work. This is only one of the reversals: on the wedding night of Russ, Mamma Aimee's brother-in-law, and Katie,

43

HUNT LIBRARY
CARNEGIE-MELLON UNIVERSITY

he had dropped blood on the marriage-bed; Negroes talk back; the preacher wants to make love with a prostitute. The novel brings together some of Caldwell's most effective themes and situations: inactive children, grotesque love, economic problems, religious dilemmas. The novel contains characters as grotesque as any in recent "gothic" fiction; yet the whole is again grandly rendered in the comic mode, as though in his full maturity Caldwell had returned to his major themes with renewed vigor.

Miss Mamma Aimee is a fine return to Caldwell's major themes and methods, as *Georgia Boy* was a brilliant recoup after the war novel. If we discount the two early novels (*The Bastard* and *Poor Fool*) Caldwell's career may be said to begin in 1930 with the publication of the collection of stories titled *American Earth.* The next decade contains his best work, including *Tobacco Road, God's Little Acre, Journeyman,* and *Trouble in July,* as well as the book of essays *Some American People,* and the text-picture books *You Have Seen Their Faces, North of the Danube,* and *Say! Is This the U.S.A.* After the war, he seemed to have difficulty in getting back into his fictional world and in creating wholly satisfying books. *Georgia Boy* in 1943 and *Complete Stories* ten years later in 1953 are the exceptions. Otherwise the later novels vary in effectiveness and quality, the most frequent fault being trite characterization and insufficient motivation. The books do contain wit and humor; they are written still in the plain style; and they have the power to make one keep turning the pages. Caldwell's technique developed during this long period, as he began to introduce parenthetical comments in italics, sometimes monologues of characters, sometimes comments from outside the story entirely. Though the novels are not wholly successful, the texture became denser. The parentheses are like those of Virginia Woolf in *To the Lighthouse* which suggest an author not omniscient, suggest that the characters have lives of their own about which the author has only hints and guesses. Caldwell's parentheses suggest that the author is reporter of objective reality, and the report is submitted to other commentators who come at the action or character from different points of view, thus reinforcing the sense of the solidity and reality of action and character. His experimentation with this technique reaches its most successful point in the more recent books, such as the novel *Miss Mamma Aimee* and the biographical *Deep South*.

Caldwell, now in such disrepute among academic critics, will one day be "discovered," and his reputation will rest on a few books. Although he is one of the American masters of the short story, many of his stories are much of a kind and many others are trivial. Yet one could make a collection of twenty-five of Caldwell's stories which would reveal his talent and which would be a minor classic of American literature, standing in relation to the giant works of our literature much as a selection of de Maupassant's stories stands in relation to French fiction. Although every reader will quarrel with a selection from a large body of short fiction, any selection would need to include such classics as "Country Full of Swedes," "Kneel to the Rising Sun," "The People *v.* Abe Lathan, Colored," "Candy-Man Beechum," and "After-Image." Some of the stories are chillingly terrifying and seem closer to more recent visions of terror and absurdity than to the times in which they were first published. "The Growing Season," for instance, is a story in a remarkably contemporary manner. A farmer, beaten down first by rain and then by sun, gets his shotgun, and in a moment of violent frustration and rage at the ways of nature and of man, he slaughters Fiddler. Even a respected and perceptive scholar-critic like Joseph Warren Beach said that "the negro Jesse . . . cannot bear to witness the suffering of his donkey; he shoots the animal and goes on sharpening the blade of his hoe." Yet clearly that is not what

45

happens in the story. Fiddler is not a donkey, a mule, or an old hound-dog. The vision in "The Growing Season" is as ironic, as black, as any in contemporary fiction. Yet the range of attitude and emotion in Caldwell's stories is wide. "An Evening in Nuevo Leon" is absurd comedy, "The Day the Presidential Candidate Came to Ciudad Tamaulipas" is brilliant political satire, "We Are Looking at You, Agnes" is a subtle psychological sketch, and other stories are richly comic, like "An Autumn Courtship," "Meddlesome Jack," and "The Negro in the Well." To this dozen I would add "Daughter," "Hamrick's Polar Bear," "Horse Thief," "Man and Woman," "Maud Island," "A Swell-looking Girl," "Return to Lavinia," "A Woman in the House," "Yellow Girl," and "Wild Flowers."

Tobacco Road, Journeyman, and *Miss Mamma Aimee* are all good novels, though I think later readers will find his most satisfying to be *God's Little Acre* and *Georgia Boy;* and those two novels are sufficiently different in theme, attitude, and technique to give some idea of Caldwell's range. *North of the Danube* and *Say! Is This the U.S.A.* may be too expensive to keep in print, so that a selected volume of essays will form part of the standard works of the "discovered" Caldwell: the essay on Detroit, some of the essays from the text-picture books, and some chapters from the travel books. One might add parts of the loving and dutiful son's recollections of his father in *Deep South.* The book is technically a biography but is actually about a man's travels through the interior landscape of memory, together with reports of his travels in the present and of what men today are saying. Such a selection from the large and uneven body of Caldwell's writing will make clear the strength of his best work in fiction and non-fiction, and will reveal what is now obscured by the very bulk of his output: his is a solid achievement that supports the assertion that he is one of the important writers of our time.

⌐ Selected Bibliography

Principal Works of Erskine Caldwell

NOVELS

The Bastard. New York: Heron Press, 1929.
Poor Fool. New York: Rariora Press, 1930.
Tobacco Road. New York: Scribner, 1932.
God's Little Acre. New York: Viking, 1933.
Journeyman. New York: Viking, 1935.
The Sacrilege of Alan Kent. Portland, Me.: Falmouth Book House, 1936.
Trouble in July. New York: Duell, Sloan and Pearce, 1940.
All Night Long. New York: Duell, Sloan and Pearce, 1942.
Georgia Boy. New York: Duell, Sloan and Pearce, 1943.
Tragic Ground. New York: Duell, Sloan and Pearce, 1944.
A House in the Uplands. New York: Duell, Sloan and Pearce, 1946.
The Sure Hand of God. New York: Duell, Sloan and Pearce, 1947.
This Very Earth. New York: Duell, Sloan and Pearce, 1948.
Place Called Esterville. New York: Duell, Sloan and Pearce, 1949.
Episode in Palmetto. New York: Duell, Sloan and Pearce, 1950.
A Lamp for Nightfall. New York: Duell, Sloan and Pearce, 1952.
Love and Money. New York: Duell, Sloan and Pearce, 1954.
Gretta. Boston: Little, Brown, 1955.
Claudelle Inglish. Boston: Little, Brown, 1958.
Jenny by Nature. New York: Farrar, Straus and Cudahy, 1961.
Close to Home. New York: Farrar, Straus and Cudahy, 1962.
The Last Night of Summer. New York: Farrar, Straus, 1963.
Miss Mamma Aimee. New York: New American Library, 1967.
Summertime Island. New York and Cleveland: World, 1968.

COLLECTIONS OF STORIES

American Earth. New York: Scribner, 1930.
We Are the Living. New York: Viking, 1933.
Kneel to the Rising Sun. New York: Viking, 1935.
Southways. New York: Viking, 1938.
Jackpot. New York: Duell, Sloan and Pearce, 1940.
The Courting of Susie Brown. New York: Duell, Sloan and Pearce, 1952.
Complete Stories. Boston: Little, Brown, 1953.
Gulf Coast Stories. Boston: Little, Brown, 1956.
Certain Women. Boston: Little, Brown, 1957.
When You Think of Me. Boston: Little, Brown, 1959.

NONFICTION

Tenant Farmers. New York: Phalanx Press, 1935.
Some American People. New York: McBride, 1935.
Moscow under Fire. London: Hutchinson, 1942.
All-Out on the Road to Smolensk. New York: Duell, Sloan and Pearce, 1942.
Call It Experience. New York: Duell, Sloan and Pearce, 1951.
Around about America. New York: Farrar, Straus, 1964.
In Search of Bisco. New York: Farrar, Straus and Giroux, 1965.
In the Shadow of the Steeple. London: Heinemann, 1967.
Writing in America. New York: Phaedra, 1967.
Deep South. New York: Weybright and Talley, 1968.

PICTURE-TEXTS WITH MARGARET BOURKE-WHITE

You Have Seen Their Faces. New York: Modern Age Books and Viking, 1937.
North of the Danube. New York: Viking, 1939.
Say! Is This the U.S.A. New York: Duell, Sloan and Pearce, 1941.
Russia at War. London and New York: Hutchinson, 1942.

Critical Studies

Beach, Joseph Warren. "Erskine Caldwell: The Comic Catharsis," in *American Fiction: 1920–1940.* New York: Macmillan, 1941.
Burke, Kenneth. "Caldwell: Maker of Grotesques," in *The Philosophy of Literary Form.* 2nd ed. Baton Rouge: Louisiana State University Press, 1967.
Cantwell, Robert. "Introduction" to *The Humorous Side of Erskine Caldwell.* New York: Duell, Sloan and Pearce, 1951.
Collins, Carvel. "Erskine Caldwell at Work," *Atlantic,* 202:21–27 (July 1958).
_____. "Introduction" to *Erskine Caldwell's Men and Women.* Boston: Little, Brown, 1961.
Frohock, W. M. "Erskine Caldwell: Sentimental Gentleman from Georgia," *Southwest Review,* 31:351–59 (1946).
Gossett, Louise Y. *Violence in Recent Southern Fiction.* Durham, N.C.: Duke University Press, 1965.
Hazel, Robert. "Notes on Erskine Caldwell," in *Southern Renaissance,* edited by Louis D. Rubin, Jr., and Robert D. Jacobs. Baltimore: Johns Hopkins University Press, 1953.
McIlwain, Shields. *The Southern Poor-White from Lubberland to Tobacco Road.* Norman: University of Oklahoma Press, 1939.
MacLachlan, John. "Folk and Culture in the Novels of Erskine Caldwell," *Southern Folklore Quarterly,* 9:93–101 (January 1945).